Building Confidence in Education

A Practical Approach for Principals

Lew Armistead

National Association of Secondary School Principals

Copyright 1982
NASSP

ISBN 0-88210-131-5

National Association of Secondary School Principals
1904 Association Drive • Reston, Va. 22091

THIS MONOGRAPH IS dedicated to those educators who understand the importance of their profession; who know that they hold the key to building America. It is dedicated to those who understand that we need to do the best job we can for students, and that we need to tell people about our values and accomplishments.

Contents

Foreword

RAPID TECHNOLOGICAL ADVANCES and dramatic increases in human knowledge have ensured that America's schools will play an all-important role in the coming century. In fact, the nation that places the most importance on education will almost certainly lead the rest of the world in progress during the twenty-first century.

Every survey that we have taken during the last 25 years has shown that the public would like more information about the schools and the educational system. Unfortunately, "bad" news is always on the surface, quickly available to the press. The "good" news lies buried and must be mined by aggressive and imaginative efforts.

Those who are engaged in the various professions typically make the error of assuming that the general public knows far more than they do about the goals, the problems, and the achievements of their profession. And this applies most certainly to those in the field of education.

It can't be assumed that all persons appreciate the value of education. Advertisers don't make this mistake with the products they sell. The merits of a simple and widely used product are extolled constantly and in every possible way.

An effective public relations program, like charity, must begin at home. Teachers need to do a great deal more than they presently do to emphasize the importance of education. In fact, at the beginning of each daily lesson, teachers should point out the importance to the students of what they will be taught that day.

Principals and other administrators need to remind parents of the important role that education will play in the lives of their sons and daughters. And those who are engaged in the public relations program for the schools have the more difficult, but equally important task of convincing members of the community that the schools merit their strong support.

An aggressive and carefully planned public relations program can reduce the dropout rate, induce more students to go on to higher education, and help obtain the tax revenues that are necessary for a strong school system.

By informing the public of the values and achievements of their local schools educators can ensure that schools continue to shape each new generation.

George Gallup

Introduction

NO ONE EVER SAID it would be easy.

I remember those words from my first expectant parents' class. It certainly has held true in raising children, but the speaker might just as well have been talking about building public confidence in our schools. That task isn't easy either. Education is so important, however, that no matter how difficult the task, it can be rewarding.

One important component of our daily activities is school communications—sharing information about the job we are doing with students. This monograph provides some public relations ideas that you can use tomorrow. It also discusses some theories about communications and explains how you are developing an image for your school, whether you know it or not.

The pronoun "you" is used frequently in this monograph for an important reason. **You** are the key to building a positive image for your school and for education. No one has a greater chance to build public understanding of schools than the principal, headmaster, or assistant principal. This monograph will provide you with some ideas that can be implemented in your school. But it's up to **you.**

You will not find all the answers here, and all the suggestions may not be appropriate for your school. Evaluate them and decide what will work best for you. Each suggestion is marked with 🍎.

And don't try to implement all of these ideas tomorrow. They will take some time, so start with a few now. Do them well and expansion of your public relations program can follow.

The aim of school public relations is to create public support for your program. By devoting some time to these activities now you will save time in the long run. If your community understands what is happening in your school, you will receive fewer questions based on misinformation or misunderstanding.

You can build the public's confidence in your schools and in education. No one said it would be easy, but it is necessary and it can be gratifying. Good luck!

*   *   *   *

Acknowledgments and thanks are sincerely expressed to the many school public relations professionals who have shared ideas, many of which are related in this monograph.

1. The Importance of Communications in Education

IF A NATION EXPECTS to be ignorant and free, in a state of civilization, it expects what never was and never will be."

The thoughts of some advertising genius, or perhaps the president of an educational association? Wrong on both counts. That was the appraisal of Thomas Jefferson when this country was developing a most unusual form of government—democracy—and a new idea—universal education.

Jefferson knew the importance of both and realized they were tied closely together. If the people of a nation were to form a union governed by the people, they would have to be an educated people, knowledgeable enough to make wise decisions. The schools would carry a grave responsibility in such a system of government—the responsibility to create that educated group of people.

Jefferson was not the only early proponent of a strong education system. When running for the Illinois State Assembly in 1832, Abraham Lincoln announced, "Upon the subject of education . . . I can only say that I view it as the most important subject which we as a people can be engaged in."

James Conant, former president of Harvard University, wrote: "Historians will regard the American high school, as it was perfected in the Twentieth Century, as not only one of the finest products of democracy, but as a continuing insurance for the preservation of the vitality of a society of free men."

Today opinions about schools and education differ dramatically. Californians in 1976 passed the sweeping Proposition 13 agreeing, apparently, with its initiator Howard Jarvis, that "The only difference between public education and the Mafia is that public education steals more money." Two years later, 10 states had a similar measure on their ballots. School board members, once viewed as providing an important community service, now face frequent recall elections.

What has brought about this distrust of schools and educators? Why do people doubt an educational system that is providing more schooling for more citizens than ever before? Have those of us in education made some mistake?

The answer to the latter is probably "yes." Too many principals, teachers, school board members, professional support personnel, and central office administrators have felt for too long that all they needed to do was teach students well. Achieve that, they reasoned, and education would continue to rest at the pinnacle of public opinion.

If educators were to make a mistake, that supposition was a significant one. There's no question that serving students, both young and old, is our most important responsibility. But in some ways we have let our society pass us by. Today we live in an image-oriented land. Marketing is a key concept.

People are told through the mass media what to eat, how to entertain themselves, what to drive, and where to go on vacation. We as educators must realize that we have a responsibility to our profession—and to the entire structure of the American way of life—to promote education. If we don't do it, some tax crusaders will do it for us. It's that simple.

John Wherry, executive director of the National School Public Relations Association (NSPRA), summed up our dilemma when he said, "We are accustomed to guarantees in America. New car manufacturers vie with each other to see who can offer the most attractive warranties. We are urged to buy 'lifetime' automobile mufflers and batteries. TV sets, transistor radios, electronic games, cameras—everything has a guarantee.

"Even our U.S. Constitution provides guarantees: freedom of speech, freedom of the press, freedom of religion, freedom of assembly. And our Declaration of Independence sets forth the principle that every citizen is entitled to life, liberty, and the pursuit of happiness.

"But strange as it may seem, there is absolutely no guarantee anywhere that our U.S. system of free public education will continue into the twenty-first century."

Wherry is right. There is no guarantee.

It is our job to create a guarantee. We must let the public know that our schools are doing their job, that schools deserve their support.

The task is not impossible. We *can* build public confidence in education. The following chapters will suggest some important resources for improving our image, along with some low-cost public relations activities.

But first, perhaps we need to answer the question, "Why bother to communicate?"

The Importance of Communication

There are many reasons to inform all of our publics about education. For example:

- Taxpayers deserve to know how their dollars are spent.
- Parents entrust us with their most prized possession—their children—and they deserve to know how we are educating them.
- Community members should understand the achievements of their schools.

Those reasons are enough to justify communication today. But three other reasons for communication might be even more appropriate, considering the challenges now facing education:

- For Survival
- For Students
- For Our Sanity.

For survival. Education is truly facing the question of survival. If education loses, its demise may be slow, by means of the tax-cutting approach we are seeing in many states, or it may be by a more rapid method, such as one that almost occurred in California in 1979, when an initiative was circulated. In part, it read: "Neither the state government nor any of its creations shall engage in the operation or regulation of elementary, secondary, or technical schools."

It didn't qualify for the ballot, but if it had, and if it had passed, it would have literally outlawed public education in the largest state in the country.

Will we see similar measures in other states? No one can be certain, but such measures are much more likely to appear if people do not understand the value of education.

For students. Cities and neighborhoods can offer many resources to our young people, including a large cadre of volunteers with special skills and expertise; businesses that could provide on-the-job learning opportunities; and community organizations and private enterprises able to provide scholarships for young adults. That great pool of resources will never be fully tapped in any community, however, until that community becomes familiar with and supportive of its schools. The more information we can provide about our schools, the more likely these opportunities will be provided for students.

For our sanity. Finally, let's simply think of our mental state for a moment. More educators are feeling down in the dumps about working in schools than ever before. We see "burnout" and early retirement. We see talented professionals leaving education to find work in other areas. We are tired of being criticized because we have devoted our lives to serving young people. Until we build public confidence, however, we will continue to face that criticism.

Communicating about schools and subsequently building support for education may not be easy, but it can be done. It's important for our democracy, our economy, our self-defense, and our students. It needs to be done.

It's up to all of us.

2. What Is School Public Relations?

EVERY SCHOOL HAS a public relations program. Educators who think they are not involved in public relations are likely to have a very negative image in their school community.

Perhaps the key to building a positive public relations program is to understand that principals, assistant principals, and teachers don't have the choice of becoming involved in school public relations. They already are.

The clearest example of this comes at the elementary school level, where each day many students go home after school to be greeted by anxious parents. As soon as the child enters the house, the question rings out, "What did you learn in school today?" In many homes the answer comes just as quickly, "Nothin'." That is public relations.

The easiest definition of school public relations may be "what people think of the experiences at your school." And there are many ways those opinions are formed. What we, as educators who are concerned about our image, must remember is that we cannot decide not to have a public relations program. Students, parents, and the media representatives are always going to report school events. We cannot forbid them to do so. We can, however, help to assure that most of those reports are positive instead of negative by building a public relations program that will produce a positive image.

In defining school public relations perhaps one initial step is to look at what it is not. The most important thing to remember is that *public relations is not a way to cover up mistakes.* There is no substitute for doing a good job. If you make a mistake on Monday afternoon, you can't "fix it" by sending out a news release on Tuesday morning. People carry your messages; how you treat them will, to a great extent, determine that message.

NSPRA Executive Director John Wherry says there are four things educators must accomplish if the American people are to support their schools:

1. Do a good job.
2. Do a Good Job.
3. DO A GOOD JOB.
4. Be sure people know about it.

That makes it sound simple, but it also is an accurate description of

5

our task. If we don't do a good job all the news releases, annual reports, and speeches will be for naught.

We should also remember to speak English when we communicate with the public. We all went through those many hours of educational theory classes where we were exposed to such concepts as the affective and cognitive domains, but this is not the time to speak "educationese." This is the time to communicate in terms that everyone will understand. Forget about vertical articulation when talking with a community member, conducting a parent-teacher conference, or speaking at an open house.

Remember, there are two components to the communication process: a sender and a receiver. The important component is the receiver. If the receiver can't understand our message, our efforts have been in vain.

Public relations does not have to take a great deal of time. We need to practice a few activities consistently to build confidence in schools, but it's not necessary to spend eight hours a day working on image-building activities. School public relations is in many ways a common sense activity, as will be discussed in Chapter 7.

Key Components of School PR

The National School Public Relations Association defines school public relations as "a planned and systematic two-way process of communications between an educational organization and its internal and external publics. Its program serves to stimulate a better understanding of the role, objectives, accomplishments, and needs of the organization. Educational public relations is a management function that interprets public attitudes, identifies the policies and procedures of an individual organization with the public interest, and executes a program of action to encourage public involvement and to earn public understanding and acceptance." That definition includes some key words: *planned, systematic, two-way.*

Planning. In building a public relations program that has a positive outcome, it is crucial to plan. Positive public relations is that which is planned; destructive public relations is that which just happens. The third grade student's answer to that well-known question, "What did you learn at school?" may not be planned and can result in a very negative image. If you think that third graders are likely to report what happens in school, you can imagine the impact a high school sophomore's response might have. Planning will be a key element discussed later in this monograph.

Two-way communications. Two-way communication is also critical. We must listen to what the community has to say about its schools. Listening is important if for no other reason than to save us time and money. There is not enough money available in education today to waste any of it, whether it be on communications or any other activity in our schools. It's important to listen to what people ask, to what they say, so we can determine what their information needs are.

One way to pinpoint those information needs is to ask the school secretary to tabulate the nature of incoming phone calls for one month so that you can identify the most frequently asked questions about your school. If you discover that during one month three questions are asked about the math program and 39 about your sex education class, you have an idea what people want to know. Now find ways to communicate information on that topic.

Honesty. School public relations must also be an honest activity. We must always tell the truth or our credibility will be destroyed.

A good illustration is found in a situation that occurred during a school district strike, when the superintendent went before the television cameras and announced, "We may have a strike in our district, but school is going on as usual." That evening the nightly news show used his statement in its entirety, and then showed footage from the local high school where 50 percent of the classrooms had no teachers, and where students were jumping out of windows and running up and down the hallways. The message delivered by the superintendent to his community was that the film depicted the district's "usual" learning program.

We should be willing to admit our weaknesses and to openly discuss the constraints that we face in education. This goes hand in hand with communicating what we do well. In discussing weaknesses or problems we should always emphasize where improvement is necessary, what steps are being taken to improve, and what parents and the community at large can contribute to the improvement efforts.

For example, if people are asking for more programs when funds are dwindling, educators should mention the budgetary situation and discuss ways to obtain the necessary money for the desired additional programs. You can be sure that news about school problems will reach the community. Problems cannot be hidden.

Common sense. School public relations is common sense in dealing with people. What we call public relations (pr) might be better termed rp—relating with people. Educators have the opportunity to meet with many people, including students, parents, volunteers, and community leaders. Each of these meetings is an opportunity to build support for schools, provided educators use a little common sense and treat these people well.

Dealing with perceptions. Another key concept in school public relations is dealing with the perceptions your publics hold, because sometimes they can be more important than facts. This concept can be explained best through another example.

7

Community members in one school district were concerned about school discipline problems. Rumors spread about poor discipline in the schools, letters to the editor of the local newspaper pointed out bad conduct, and adults stormed the governing board meetings seeking an end to "lax discipline."

The principals, teachers, and district administrators huddled, but couldn't recall any major behavior problems except a few fights among students. The educators didn't believe that there was a discipline problem in their secondary schools. But how could they communicate that to the public?

The educators could have stood by their opinion that discipline was good in the schools, and sent that message through newsletters, speeches, and discussions at meetings. But the community already *perceived* that discipline was poor.

Instead, the educators decided to dust off the district discipline policy, take it to a board meeting, and update it in just a few places. Taking that public action indicated to community members that the educators were also concerned about discipline and were "doing something about it." Community members felt much better after something had been done about their perceptions.

Implementing school public relations is like other projects in schools. We need to plan objectives, build a program, provide staff development, evaluate efforts, and plan ways to improve for the following year.

The final goal of any educational public relations project is to build support for the school. You will never eliminate all the negative messages, because education is filled with human beings, and human beings don't always see things the same way. But by planning, encouraging staff development, and spending a little time each week on school public relations, you can communicate many more positive messages than negative ones. That should be your goal: to have more pluses than minuses when everything is totaled.

We must remember that positive public relations is planned; negative public relations just happens.

3. Who Communicates, And What Should They Say?

SCHOOL COMMUNICATIONS HAS been called a family affair, and that certainly is the case when one looks at all the people who send messages for a school. Perhaps no other single activity involves such a cross section of individuals.

Two general publics are served by a secondary school—an internal public and an external one. The internal group consists of those people most closely connected with the school: students, teachers, support staff, parents, volunteers, central office administrators, and members of the board of education. External audiences are more diverse and can be more difficult to identify. They might include adults without children in the schools, civic clubs, churches, senior citizen groups, the city council, reporters, editors, realtors, local representatives to Congress and the state legislature, the chamber of commerce, taxpayer associations, homeowner groups, youth organizations, and business leaders.

These different publics are all important, although some may be more vocal, and their information needs may vary. It is important that all schools identify the publics in their community and plan ways to communicate with them. This can be done by brainstorming at a staff meeting or with a group representing parents, staff, and students. This is a first step in building a communications plan.

Just as there are different publics that a school must inform, there are different sources of information. Surveys indicate that students, newspapers, school staff members, and parents of students are major sources of school news.

Sources of News About Schools

One of the most important publics for principals and assistant principals is the parents. But their numbers are decreasing. A decade ago, about half of the adults in the United States had children in school. Today only about one-fourth of the adult population have children in school. That means fewer people have a way to receive information about schools and education on a daily basis. While students are still a very important source of news, educators must reach out to other sources.

Students. There are fewer students today, but they continue to be a valued source of information, especially to parents:

- A 1980 statewide survey in Mississippi indicated that students were the most popular single source of information about schools for both parents and the general public. Parents reported that 22 percent of their information came from students, 13 percent from school employees, 11 percent from family, 9 percent from newspapers, 8 percent each from parents of students and parent groups, and 7 percent from personal involvement. The general public indicated that 20 percent of its information about schools came from students, 12 percent from school employees, and 11 percent from newspapers.
- A similar survey in Ohio found that the general public's second most used information source about schools was school-aged children, outranked only by newspapers.
- Students were the number one source of information (26 percent) reported by Brevard County (Fla.) parents in a 1978 poll. In that same survey, students were the top source reported by the general public (21 percent) and the second most used source by nonparents (17 percent).
- In a 1981 survey conducted in the Tulsa (Okla.) Public Schools newsletter, 63 percent of the readers—primarily parents—reported that their children were the source of the most information about their schools.

So even with the declining student population, students continue to be a prime source of information about education. It's interesting to note that not only do students directly affect the opinion parents develop about schools, but in so doing, students also are affecting the information parents will communicate to others. Parents of students were the third most used source of information in the Brevard County survey.

School staff members. Another extremely important source of news is the school staff. School employees were the second most used information source by parents and the general public in the Mississippi survey, and first among legislators.

Volunteers. One frequently used source of information is volunteers. This group has an important advantage in the eyes of many audiences—credibility. Many people view volunteers as having a personal involvement in schools without the "bias" of being employed by the school district. Volunteers include PTA members, classroom and library aides, and band and football boosters.

Media. Aside from "people communicators," newspapers fare the best. They were the main source of information among respondents in a 1979 Springfield, Mo., survey; the Ohio poll; and a 1981 Fairfax County, Va. survey. In areas where people have less contact with the schools, including those locales with fewer parents, newspapers are a very important communication vehicle. Most recent surveys show that radio and television are not major sources of news about local schools. Two exceptions were the Tulsa poll, where they ranked third and fourth among eight choices; and the Springfield, Mo., survey where television was the third most used information source. The electronic media may become more important information vehicles as educators learn to work more closely with them.

School publications are another important source of school news. They ranked as the fourth most cited single source in the Springfield poll; third in the Ohio survey; second in the Fairfax County study; and first among parents in East Lansing, Mich., according to a 1980 survey.

While certain sources of information rise to the top in polls, these recent school surveys show that there are a variety of potential sources. It's best to evaluate which are most effective in your community and to make sure enough different sources are used to reach all your audiences. For example, a school newsletter may be very effective in communicating with parents, but is not likely to get into the hands of senior citizens.

Making Sources Effective Communicators

The surveys indicate that students, school staff members, parents, and volunteers communicate messages for schools. You cannot turn that communication off and on like a water faucet. People will always send messages about your school. But you can help make those messages more positive than negative, and that is the key to building an effective school communications program.

It is crucial that potential communicators have accurate, up-to-date information and possess a good feeling about their relationship with education. A person who is not informed obviously cannot answer questions. Someone who is uncomfortable with his or her experiences in your school is not likely to communicate positive messages. Let's look at some ways communicators can be given information and good feelings about the school.

Some students, especially those who have been involved in school activities, are fairly knowledgeable about the school routine. But you must try to inform all students, including those who hang out behind the gym, litter the neighboring lawn with ice cream wrappers, and don't attend all their classes. Those young people also have a sphere of influence, parents who ask questions, and neighbors who want to know about schools.

There are a number of standard ways to communicate with students, such as the school newspaper and morning announcements. These can be effective, but you should always seek ways to improve these vehicles.

An art instructor at one school who happened also to be an opera buff felt that students really weren't listening to the morning announcements, which were read by the teacher in each first period class. One day he gave up reading the announcements and performed them in operatic style. Students listened. Some even complimented him on his voice. That is an idea that worked for one teacher and obviously wouldn't work everyplace. But it's the kind of creativity that leads to a positive communications program.

11

Some schools that rely on a public address system to deliver announcements have found ways to encourage greater attention. Playing music before and after the announcements, or using news of interest to students will help. Such items could include sports scores, announcements of upcoming dances, special events, etc. Students are a great source of information on how to improve school announcements. Ask them.

A school newspaper can be a good communications vehicle. Principals should establish a good rapport with the staff members and always be accessible to them. Discuss important messages with the editor of the paper. A school radio station can also be an effective information tool.

One high school principal established a school communications council. The group, which met about once a month, included representatives of all segments of the student body. The principal discussed such topics as the school budget, new rules, and reasons a certain course could not be offered, and encouraged the students to share that information with their peers. He also devoted a portion of each session to finding out what concerned students and what their information needs were.

Just as important as informing students is making them feel good about being in their school. Be sure to call students by their first names, congratulate them on academic and activity successes, and honor student groups for special achievements. There are many ways to build a positive relationship with your young people. Remember, it is an important part of the school public relations program.

The school staff members constitute another important group of communicators. They, too, must be informed and enthusiastic about the school if they are to be positive communicators. The typical ways of informing staff—bulletins, meetings, or get-togethers—are effective if they are frequent and provide useful information. There are also many ways to congratulate staff, and that should be a priority for all school administrators. In one school system in Ohio, whenever the superintendent discovers that a staff member has accomplished something special, he sends a congratulatory note. A principal or assistant principal could easily adopt such a practice.

A special group should be mentioned here. When some educators think of staff, they envision the teachers and forget the support staff members. Secretaries, custodians, cafeteria workers, bus drivers, aides, and other school employees are important sources of information. In fact, a number of surveys have indicated that these people are the most used sources for information about the school. The custodian may be the only person at school to greet a visitor after 4:30. The secretary is the first to answer the phone, and the bus driver may be the last school staff member to deal with students before they return home each day.

Although these individuals are very important to a school's communications program, they are sometimes overlooked when it is time to receive news. Ensure that all staff members are knowledgeable about education and school happenings.

Volunteers are another group sometimes neglected in a school's information program. People in your community may question the president of the band boosters club about the school instead of asking a teacher, secretary, or assistant principal; thus, it's important that key volunteers are knowledgeable about schools. Perhaps they should receive the staff bulletin or be invited to informational meetings.

It's also important that volunteers have a good feeling about their involvement. If they are to be positive communicators, they should feel satisfied. One principal who has about 150 volunteers in his school, takes the time twice a year to write each one a personal thank you note. On the top of the postcard he uses is printed, "There are 10 good reasons why we appreciate you—here's one of them." The principal then writes a brief note. This is very time consuming, but the principal believes it helps to create 150 positive communicators for his school.

There are many other ways to say "thank you"—certificates, a luncheon, recognition at a game or concert, or an article in the school newsletter. Remember, saying thank you has an impact on the image of your school. Information and positive attitudes can help build a positive communications program.

What Does Everyone Want To Know?

The information people want about schools varies, depending on their interests. Generally, parents seek knowledge about instruction; taxpayers without children are interested in the way money is spent; and teachers may want clarification of the discipline policy. It's important that the school team identify its publics and what each needs to know.

A 1980 East Lansing, Mich., poll indicated that 27 percent of the parents and guardians sought greater knowledge about curriculum; 13 percent wanted to know more about their child's progress; and 12 percent wanted more information about teachers and teaching methods. In the Mississippi survey, 14 percent of the parents desired more news about curriculum and 13 percent about the qualifications of teachers. Those two choices, in reverse order, were also the greatest information needs of the general public. Academic standards, special instructional programs, administration, budget, teaching methods, and discipline also ranked high on the list.

Polls provide a general direction, but there's no substitute for determining specific information needs. Spend 20 minutes in your next staff meeting brainstorming the information needs of your three largest publics. Ask your PTA, advisory council, or football booster club members to complete a short form outlining information needs. A mini-community survey could be taken by a senior government, journalism, or sociology class. You can effectively determine what your community wants to know.

Read that last sentence again. It is crucial to an effective school communications program. Educators must deliver information that interests the public. You cannot only communicate news you want your community to have. Certainly, schools have some very important messages that must be shared, but in addition you need to answer community members' questions. If you communicate only the news you want known, your publics will soon stop listening.

What about the bad news? You shouldn't try to communicate only the rosy news about your school. But, when a challenge or problem is discussed, communications should focus on what is being done to repair the problem and how others can help to improve the situation. Don't try to hide the problem. If you openly communicate ways you are dealing with it, you will earn the respect of your community.

14

4. Traditional
Public Relations Vehicles

MANY PUBLIC INFORMATION TOOLS that have been used for years are still effective today. These are dealt with in this chapter. With any school public relations idea, however, one caution must be kept in mind. All of the following ideas have been used successfully somewhere, but they might not be the most practical ones for your school or community. You know your community best. Evaluate these ideas and decide what will work best for you.

There are two general ways to communicate, and each has its separate advantages and disadvantages. *Mass communication* techniques include news releases, bulletins, and newsletters. They are effective in reaching a large number of people quickly. Parent-teacher conferences and school meetings are *interpersonal communications* techniques. They are most effective in changing attitudes, since they provide the opportunity for asking questions and dealing with the specific concerns of the individual. But it's difficult to reach a large number of people through an interpersonal technique. Likewise, it may be hard to alter someone's attitude through a mass communications approach. Each school should plan to use both methods to achieve its communications objectives.

Newspapers

Every community is served by a newspaper, whether it is a weekly, small daily, or metropolitan paper. The newspapers in your area provide a quick, low-cost way to reach large numbers of people.

Many Americans, especially adults without children in school, rely on newspapers for their education news. They certainly are a part of any school's public relations program. The press can be the friend of an educator, as is discussed in Chapter 8, but there is much more to building an effective relationship with the media than issuing news releases. But for now, let's see how principals and assistant principals can obtain newspaper coverage.

The best route is by working through the school district public information professionals. They will have the writing skills and the press contacts to help obtain coverage. If your district is not so fortunate as to have such a person, there is no reason why news releases cannot be sent from the school. "The World's Shortest Course in Educational Journalism" on page 44 gives you a quick guide to preparing news releases. Be sure all newspapers get the same information at the same time.

You can also obtain coverage for some stories by phoning the editor or reporter at the paper and encouraging them, for example, to interview students and/or teachers involved in a new course. They won't want to cover everything at your school, but are likely to respond to some good suggestions.

What makes a good newspaper story? Reporters generally are looking for something that is timely and new. Something that is different, such as senior citizens attending high school classes, is always a possibility. Events that include a large number of students or other people also have press potential.

The following are potential stories if they are happening at your school:

- Student awards in speech contests, science fairs, industrial arts contests, or scholarship competitions—anything that makes your students look good shows the accomplishments of your school.
- New trends in instruction. The introduction of computers to the curriculum, or a new learning philosophy.
- Ways that a local school is responding to national education concerns such as discipline or test scores. Is your school raising its performance on SATs?
- Everything visual. The Spanish class' lunchtime festival, complete with simulated bullfights.
- Peer tutoring. Are your students working in elementary school classrooms?
- Senior citizen involvement in schools. Are long-time community residents teaching mini-lessons on local history? Is your foods class preparing a lunch for senior citizens?
- Visits by foreign groups or exchange students.
- Student participation in city government day, or visits to a legislator's office.
- Student involvement in the community. Is your science class cleaning up a dry creek bed? Are members of the chorus or gymnastics team performing at a local club?
- Parent or other adult involvement. Is your PTA or home-school club taking a stance on an important issue? Is the school presenting an award to a volunteer for dedicated service?
- Unusual instructional programs. Does a science class maintain an ecology area with chickens and goats? Do you have a school radio station that broadcasts into the community?
- Milestones, both for the school and school personnel. Has a custodian worked in the school for more than 25 years?
- Special exhibits. Are your art students presenting an exhibit at a local shopping center or in the school?
- Vocational education classes. Are some of your students working in the community?

- Teacher-student switch days. Do high school students exchange places with youth in the feeder junior high or middle school? Do teachers do the same thing?

Many of these activities could develop into stories for your local newspapers, but only if you tell the reporter about them. It would be worth a phone call.

Principals and assistant principals should see that stories are sent to the press whenever students or staff members earn recognition. That is one of the best ways to show your community that students are successful and that staff members are competent.

Radio and Television

When many of us think about press coverage, newspapers generally are the first medium that comes to mind. But radio and television stations also can fit into a school's information program by providing free air time for public service announcements.

What is an appropriate public service announcement (PSA)? Upcoming school events that are open to the general public, deadlines for scholarship exams, important meetings at the school, ways that the community can become involved in the school, adult education opportunities . . . all of these would be potential PSAs.

Most stations will be happy to produce the spot from information you provide, or even record the principal or a student making the announcement. But these opportunities will not become available to your school unless you seek them. Pick up the phone and ask.

While PSAs are one way to obtain coverage on the electronic media, don't overlook news broadcasts. Radio can be especially helpful to educators, because most radio stations feature short hourly or even twice hourly news segments that include some local news. They may be very interested in news from the local middle school or high school. Again, it would be wise to pick up the phone and ask the news director about possible coverage.

Television will be much more selective in covering school events for its news shows, but don't give up hope. Anything that is visual has possibilities. Determine which courses are the most likely to interest television reporters. Science classes and vocational programs are possibilities. Again, phone the news director and see if he or she is interested.

The preceding is a brief look at getting coverage from the press, but there's much more to dealing with reporters and editors—enough to require an entire chapter, which starts on page 41.

17

Newsletters

The school newsletter tends to be a very well-read publication. A 1980 survey of parents in the East Lansing, Mich., Public Schools indicated that 80 percent of them got their information about schools from notes, memos, newsletters, or other publications from the schools.

Forty-two percent of the parents in a 1974 Fairfax County, Va., survey indicated they received most of their news from school publications.

Some tips for principals and assistant principals to remember in preparing newsletters are: write frequently; communicate in language the general public will understand; and describe items that will interest readers.

Too many educators have developed the habit of communicating only when they need something from their community. For instance, a newsletter explaining the school district's financial situation, will appear two weeks before a tax election. Or, newsletters of explanation will be distributed one week before a school is to be closed due to declining enrollment. Under those circumstances the public may ask the question, "Are they communicating with me only when they want something?" It's best to develop an ongoing schedule of newsletters, rather than sending one out only when a crisis is about to hit.

It's also best at the secondary school level to mail newsletters home. Once you have devoted your energy and dollars to printing the publication, you don't want to see 75 percent of the copies resting in the nearest trash can.

 A lack of funds doesn't necessarily have to stop a school from publishing a newsletter. As educational budgets become tighter and tighter, more and more schools look to local business and industry for support. A business might be willing to contribute to your newsletter or pay for it entirely in return for a short mention as the sponsor. (Be sure district legal or philosophical constraints do not apply.)

 One final thing to remember about school newsletters: take a few minutes to let someone else read your words. One elementary school parent recalls the time when a school newsletter announcing a PTA membership drive arrived. The principal wrote, "Our PTA membership campaign is about to begin, and all parents will receive a form. We encourage you to join PTA. Children returning their parents' membership form will receive one point in the classroom ice cream contest."

That was the end of his note, a message he really didn't intend to convey. It indicated that the only reason to join PTA was because of the ice cream contest. If he had let another person on the staff read the material before it was sent, he would have saved much time and embarrassment. Giving someone the responsibility to read and critique newsletter material can be a good step, especially if you can find someone who knows the community.

Staff Bulletins

Staff bulletins are perhaps the most important form of school communications. They are the prime way to keep all of your staff members informed of current happenings. They do not need to be fancy, but they should be frequent and available to all staff members, and should deal with information those people want to know.

Some principals have expanded the distribution list of their staff bulletin to include people other than those working at school—the PTA president, chairperson of an advisory group, the football boosters club members, and the local newspaper editor. If your staff bulletin is appropriate for such broad distribution it is a great way to inform more people without adding appreciable costs.

There are many interpersonal devices in addition to the mass communications vehicles just described. They are the ones that are most useful in changing an individual's attitudes.

Open Houses and Parent-Teacher Conferences

An open house certainly isn't a new idea, but it's a great way for parents to meet the teachers and learn about the school. Our challenge is to find new and creative ways to invite parents to attend meetings. Unfortunately, many parents look forward to going to open houses about as much as they enjoy witnessing the arrival of melons at the local supermarket.

The best way to determine what will encourage parents to attend open houses is to ask a small sample of parents what would interest them. (The sample should include all spectrums of your parent community—not just your PTA president, mother of the student body president, and president of the band boosters.)

Students can be a big selling factor when it comes to parent attendance at school events. If you can communicate the importance of open houses to your students and encourage them to recruit parental attendance, your success rate should improve. Schools could include students in the open house or provide specific events during open house that would encourage students to come with their parents.

You might begin the evening with student entertainment, or a spaghetti meal. Your chorus, band, or foods class can be a big boost to any gathering of this type.

Key Communicators

Every community has a group of individuals who are asked questions about everything. They are queried about city government, local churches, rising prices, the weather, and—yes—the local high school. These are individuals whom other people respect. They are your key communicators.

One of the strongest proponents of using key communicators is Don Bagin, 1981-1982 president of the National School Public Relations Association. He contends, "The man on the street does not generally accept or reject an idea until he talks with those people in the community whose opinion and judgment he respects." Bagin's discussion of key communicators appears at the end of this chapter.

Educators need to develop ways to keep the key communicators informed. This might include inviting them to school events such as an awards assembly, a musical, a basketball game, or a PTA meeting. It might also mean placing their names on the mailing list for your school newsletter or other mailings.

One school district brought its key communicators together as a communications committee. That group met twice a year, once in the fall and again in spring. School personnel discussed the goals of the instructional program, progress students were making, and the rationale for major decisions. District people were available to answer questions.

That idea can easily be adopted at the school level. People could be brought in for a luncheon meeting with food prepared and served by a home economics class. If key communicators are informed, they will carry a school's message into the community. This can be a fairly inexpensive way to communicate.

Students in the Community

Many secondary schools gain a tremendous image boost when talented students perform in the community. Students benefit from the opportunity to perform, and the community benefits from their performance.

We should, however, think of the many different approaches. Some secondary schools send their gymnastics teams to convalescent hospitals, art students to conduct mini-workshops at senior citizen centers, and the madrigal chorus to Rotary Club luncheons. Student artwork can be offered for displays at any number of businesses, public agencies, and local clubs.

The more exposure we can give our very talented students and their work, the greater the school's image will be.

Key Communicators—An Information Network

Don Bagin

No community is exempt from the effects of rumors that have gotten out of hand. And, in many cases, such rumors result in problems for school administrators. Usually the rumors can quickly be put to rest; but, when unchecked, they may cause what was a spark to become a raging fire.

This is the time for "key communicators."

What kind of a person should be a key communicator? Any person who talks with a large number of people should be considered for key communicator designation. A person who is believed and trusted by large numbers of people should definitely be asked to serve. The person need not have the usual formal power structure kind of status that we too often seek for school help. The person might be a barber, a beautician, or a bartender. The person might own a hoagie shop or be a school crossing guard, a postmaster, or a gas station operator.

It's important to identify key communicators who will talk with every segment of the community.

What can happen without key communicators? An example: Ten people appeared at the superintendent's office. They brought a petition signed by 1,200 people—a petition protesting the plans to bus children from that district (which was upper-middle class) to a nearby city school district. They brought reporters and a TV cameraman with them. The superintendent was surprised, as he had no inkling that there was such community concern. In fact, he did not know that the petition was being circulated.

The media, of course, had a page-one story, even though the superintendent candidly denied that any such plans had been discussed. (And this was the truth.) One person had misconstrued a statement made by another school official, and the rumor spread. Not one of the 1,200 people signing the petition talked with anyone from the school to get the facts. Everyone, it appears, assumed the petition statement was correct.

Key communicators could have informed the district of the community's concern.

Here are two examples of how the key communicators idea works:

- On the night of the senior prom, a senior was seen trying to climb the left field wall of the high school baseball field, at midnight, in his tux. This was considered unusual behavior for that community, and the rumors would probably have had the entire class on an LSD trip.

  The key communicators were told that although this student was on drugs, he was the only student under their influence. They

21

Don Bagin is professor and communications coordinator, graduate program in school public relations, Glassboro (N.J.) State College.

communicated that fact to the rest of the community, thereby avoiding what could have been a major problem for school administrators and for students throughout the district.

- The day before a tax levy election in a county school district, the county newspaper ran an accurate article that was given a page-one position. The article described the district's needs in a fair manner, but the headline was totally misleading.

School officials didn't have time to prepare a formal response of any kind. Furthermore, they did not want to alienate the newspaper by complaining about the poor headline.

Key communicators came into play by spreading the word that the news story and its salient points were excellent, but that the headline was misleading. Facts were provided to the key communicators, showing how the headline was inconsistent with the facts in the story.

Does the key communicator idea work for school, for districts, or should it be set up on a school basis? Both ways work. Some school districts identify key communicators through the superintendent's office. In this case, principals are usually asked to help select people who can serve as key communicators. In other districts, each principal is responsible for setting up a key communicator network. It is, of course, possible for superintendents to base their key communicator group on members of the principals' groups.

Should there be key communicators within the schools? Definitely. A group of student and staff key communicators can add much to the total communications effort. Study after study shows that students and staff members are prime sources of information about the schools. Therefore, it is imperative that everyone in the school know the facts before they share their information with people outside the school.

In addition to spreading the facts, how else can key communicators help? Key communicators can identify the sparks before they become fires. Members of this group must be encouraged to call school officials with questions they have, or with questions or concerns they have heard from neighbors, friends, or customers.

For example, a customer might tell Harry, the barber, that the proposed new high school is going to cost $10 million. Harry calls the superintendent and finds that the cost will be $7 million. How many people will Harry set straight? How many people will the people Harry told tell? This information network *will* help.

Some school districts call a meeting of key communicators before making a major decision. Some use the group to get ideas and reactions before presenting a budget or a bond issue to the community at large. Some get the group's thinking on issues like busing and an extended school year before going to the rest of the community.

One bonus of the system is the ability to take the pulse of the community quickly by asking the key communicators their opinions regarding almost any educational issue.

Doesn't setting up the key communicator network take time? Of course it does. In fact, most administrators are reluctant to take the time because they see it subtracting from the already limited time they have for other responsibilities. At the end of a year, however, almost all administrators agree that the key communicator network saves more time than it takes. Major crises have been averted because people get the facts before criticizing the schools.

How does a school start the key communicator idea? Several lists should be compiled, independently, by several individuals. Take a demographic look at the community to ensure that all groups are represented. Compare the original lists to determine who will be chosen. (Usually the same names appear on several lists.)

A letter should be sent to the people chosen, advising them that they have been selected and explaining the nature of the effort—to help improve schools through better communication. Invite them to a meeting with the other key communicators. A personal phone call from the principal of a school-based group, or the superintendent of a district group, usually brings from 85 percent to 95 percent attendance. The secretary's phone call usually results in about 60 percent to 75 percent attendance, and a letter of invitation only will usually attract about half the people invited.

The tone of the meeting should be informal. No formal agenda should be prepared, and the time pressures of all involved should be respected. The meeting should last 60 to 75 minutes at the longest. It should be a confidence-building session that allows people to see that the chief executive is a person who cares about students, understands that problems exist, and seems to be doing the best possible job to solve them. The administrator should make it clear that he or she is receptive to ideas and encourages questions and suggestions. People should be asked to call when they hear a rumor, and told that they will be apprised of information when a problem, challenge, or need exists.

Perhaps once a year, the entire group of key communicators should be called together for a meeting. This will enable them to see that other people in the community care enough about the school to give time to help communicate.

In an age when public confidence in public officials is low, any attempt to communicate honestly and openly will be applauded. This program can do just that. More importantly, it can help improve education.

23

5. Practical, Low-Cost Ideas For Building a Positive Image

SCHOOL NEWSLETTERS, back-to-school nights, and articles printed in local newspapers are all traditional ways to communicate. Some new ideas to consider are provided in this chapter. All have worked someplace, but you should consider whether they will work in your community. None of these ideas will cost much.

Golden Age Cards

Too often the only time a school or school district communicates with senior citizens is just prior to a tax election. Yet, those people can be a valuable resource. Senior citizens form opinions about secondary school students and communicate those opinions to others. Unfortunately, those opinions are frequently based on students racing their cars down the street and throwing litter onto someone's front lawn.

Golden age cards can bring senior citizens into the schools where they will see the positive activities of youth. The cards are provided at no cost to any senior citizen residing within the boundaries of the school or school district. The cards allow senior citizens free admission to many school activities, such as dramatic presentations, athletic events, or musicals. The school can determine what events are covered by the cards.

Volunteers

The Gallup Poll and other surveys tell us that the more personal contact an individual has with schools, the greater the level of support for education that person will show. That makes sense if the school is doing a good job.

Let people see that job firsthand. A volunteer program will bring people into the school to see what's happening, and will also provide the school with some assistance.

The group of volunteers can include a long-time resident who can discuss local history, a business person who can talk about occupational possibilities, or an individual with specific skills such as beekeeping or basketweaving who can present a mini-lesson.

Volunteer programs can increase learning opportunities for students, assist staff members, and build a positive image for your school.

Student Outreach—Student Peer Tutoring

Many elementary students experience a great deal of anxiety and uncertainty about entering secondary school. One high school has overcome that fear by having senior industrial arts students go into feeder schools and help youngsters build small, prefabricated wagons. The parts for the wagons were cut at the high school. Each senior student worked with five youngsters at a table, hammering, gluing, and assembling the wagons.

Each elementary child ended up with a wagon to take home. The youngsters, their parents, and their teachers developed positive feelings about the high schoolers. The community newspaper ran a story and photos about the project. What's more, the seniors enjoyed the activity and learned how to work with children.

Mother Nature

Mother Nature, a very dedicated secretary to a high school dean of schools, had lived in her community for 20 years and had worked at the school for 15 years. Tired of hearing negative comments about "her" school and "her" students, she decided to print a newsletter called *Mother Nature*. It had five mimeographed pages of news about student awards, staff achievements, and outstanding classroom projects. At first she gave a copy to all students and staff members. Soon, however, other community members asked for copies. Mother Nature spread a message throughout the community.

She was a person who had considerable pride in her school. If there is a potential Mother Nature on your staff it may be wise to encourage such an activity. Some schools have found a staff member or parent who likes to write, and that person has handled the school's newsletter.

School News Team

The principal or assistant principal may not be a Pulitzer Prize-calibre journalist or have the time to write stories for the local newspaper, but there may be a group of talented students in your journalism class who could write news releases about student awards, school productions, and other activities for the local papers and radio stations. It would be good experience for them and good public relations for the school. Some schools have their most experienced students work at a news bureau for the school.

The School Foods Class

The saying goes that there is no quicker way to a man's heart than through his stomach. Adapt that slightly, and you have a new public relations project. In many schools, students in the foods class eat the food as soon as they prepare it. Other students prepare meals and then serve them to adults, including senior citizens, business leaders, and other community members. A small group of people might be invited for a lunch prepared and served by students, followed by a brief discussion by the principal about the school's program and its successes. A modest charge for the meal could cover expenses.

The Speaking Circuit

Some districts conduct a speakers program as one way to communicate the school message. This idea could also be implemented in an abbreviated version at the school level.

Civic groups in every community, such as Kiwanis, women's clubs, Grange, and Rotary, are always looking for speakers for their meetings and would probably welcome a speaker from the middle level or high school. Members of these organizations represent the opinion leaders of the community, so it is important to share your message with them.

Another way to get on the speaker's circuit is via coffee klatches or meetings in homes. It is more important now than ever to tell your school's story in the community. As the number of adults with youngsters in school declines, educators need to find ways to communicate with people who don't have direct contact with schools. Speaking to various community groups is one way to achieve that.

Share That Talent

It would be hard to find a secondary school that does not contain a wealth of student talent—singers, musicians, actors, magicians, etc. Some schools, however, are very successful at keeping those talents a secret. Look for opportunities for your students to perform. They are your best good-will ambassadors. Civic clubs, senior citizen centers, shopping malls, the school board meeting—just about any community event is a possibility. Student performances are also a good way to add sparkle to some of the activities at your school, such as open houses and back-to-school nights.

Give People a Chance To Ask Questions

Some of the most inaccurate, misleading information spreads throughout a community when one person starts a rumor, so educators should look for ways to ensure that people have a chance to ask questions and have them answered. Keep in mind that some people want to remain anonymous. It is amazing how many people are timid about going into a school building, let alone a principal's office, to ask a question.

27

Some schools have developed postcards that are left in various public places. The cards have room for a question and the name, address, and phone number of the questioner. The cards can either be mailed to the school or left at a central pick-up spot. Questions are answered by mail.

Other schools advertise that an administrator will be available Friday morning between 8:00 a.m. and noon to answer telephone questions. If the administrator doesn't know the answer, the caller's name and number are taken, and a response is given within one working day.

Response systems such as these require some work, but they also go a long way toward eliminating misinformation. The key is informing the community about this service and providing enough good information so that people continue to use it.

Your Marquee and Other Public Places

How many times have you set out on a nice summer drive, passed a high school, and noticed that the marquee by the football field is promoting a game played nine months ago? That's not the case everywhere, but a better use of those announcement boards can be found in some areas.

One high school principal in Burbank, Calif., decided that his marquee would become a school communications vehicle. One spring he announced on the board: "400 students will graduate from Burbank High School. Twenty percent will receive scholarships. Twelve seniors will not graduate this year."

Shortly after the announcement appeared, the principal received a phone call from an influential attorney in town, who asked, "Do you mean that students really have to work to graduate? I thought schools simply gave social promotions." The high school diploma suddenly had meaning to this person.

Other schools communicate messages on the back of the football field press box, which faces a busy street. Barbara Kudlacek, director of public information services for the Topeka (Kans.) public schools, and William Jones, director of information services for the Philadelphia, (Pa.) School District, make use of district vehicles—such as school buses and food service trucks—to carry signs that communicate messages about the schools. The high school art and woodworking classes could produce the signs.

Yosemite (Calif.) High School at one time produced bumper stickers that read, "Happiness Is Yosemite High."

These are all ways to get your school's message to your community.

Saying "Good Job" on the Telephone

There is nothing new about teachers phoning parents and congratulating them when their students perform well. It's time to realize that those phone messages can be an important part of a school's public relations effort, and that people other than teachers can make those calls. Too often, the only time parents hear from the school is when their youngster has done something wrong—become a discipline problem or done poorly in math class. Those phone calls are important to make, but they should be balanced with positive calls.

Principals and assistant principals can encourage teachers to make those positive calls by doing it themselves. Secretaries and custodians who have contact with students can also become involved. Set a goal of calling parents. Most parents will appreciate the call, and, when calls reporting a problem have to be made the parents are more likely to support the school's actions.

28

How About a "Diploma" for Parents?

The day Johnny or Susie graduates from high school is a proud moment for Mom and Dad. It may also be the last day they have any contact with the community schools. You can make graduation an even more special time for parents.

Jeanne Magmer, coordinator of special projects for the David Douglas School District in Oregon, reports that in her district letters are sent to the parents of each graduating senior the morning after graduation. Signed by the superintendent, the letter congratulates Mom and Dad for their role in their son or daughter's graduation.

It also indicates that if this student is the last child to graduate, the school system would still like to stay in touch with them. The letter includes a card parents can use to indicate a desire to continue to receive certain publications, such as the high school newspaper, and to remain a volunteer with the district.

A School Theme or Slogan

Themes are one way to leave a message in the minds of people. If your theme is repeated often enough, people will recall it whenever they think of your school.

What could a possible theme be? How about, "Noname High School: Where Students Learn," "Noname High School: Building Our Future," "Noname High School—Everyone Learns at Noname High," or "Noname Students Are Number One." There are many possibilities.

The only guideline for such a theme is that it should be nine words or less—the shorter the better. It can be displayed on stationery; in the school office; in the school newspaper, newsletter, and PTA bulletin; on the school announcement board; and on vehicles or bumper stickers.

Bulletin Boards as PR Tools

Bulletin boards are as old as schools, yet they still can be an effective way to communicate important messages. If you have a bulletin board in the auditorium, cafeteria, or gym where members of the community will see it, consider using it to deliver important messages.

Student awards and artwork are typical items to feature on a bulletin board, but you can do much more than that. You might explain a new program in the school; you could recruit volunteers or advertise adult education opportunities; or, staff members who have been with the school for a long time or have received special recognition could be featured.

Such displays should be a combination of writing and photos or other artwork. Displays should be attractive and colorful. Ask students from an art class, journalism class, or English class to help.

Turning Students into Newspaper Celebrities

Many newspapers, especially community publications, are interested in using work by people other than staff members. A principal or

29

assistant principal could inquire whether pen-and-ink drawings, cartoons, or thoughtful essays by students might be of interest.

Getting Your Name in Print

Newspapers are including increasing numbers of reader viewpoints on their editorial pages, and guest editorials and columns are published in papers throughout the country. Your local paper might be willing to carry such a piece. The value of schools, the philosophy of your program, the achievements of students, and the need to support education are possible topics.

Communicate a School's Message

There are many ways to communicate a school's message. Ann Barkelew, public information officer for the Los Angeles County Schools and a former president of NSPRA, conducted a session on school communications at the 1981 NASSP convention. Here are a few ideas she offered that are working throughout the country. Try:

- Planning some special treatment for substitutes so they'll feel wanted, needed, and appreciated. Some schools use a Polaroid-type camera to take each sub's picture, put it up in the coffee room with a welcome message, and give it to the sub with a thank you note when he or she leaves.
- Adding a "good news" opener at the beginning of meetings. Several educators in one district now use the first 10 minutes or so for a "Did You Know" report or the sharing of "Reasons I'm Proud." Once you start it, everyone will want to get in on the act and be part of the time slot.
- Making phone calls to the homes of new students by the end of their first week of school. Principals and assistant principals who do this say they are overwhelmed by the positive response.
- Expanding "faculty meetings" to include all staff at least several times a year.
- Speaking to everyone—by name—each time you see them.
- Communicating with "feeder" schools by sharing honor rolls, newspapers, yearbooks, and the like. Little things like this build a districtwide feeling.
- Sending notes home when students show improvement.
- Doing some building-level newsletters with provocative articles and few—if any—of the traditional "principal's message" items.
- Having ready a 15 to 20-minute talk on your school or your district that you can give at meetings of all kinds. Let it be known you're available.
- Meeting regularly with student leaders to update them on achievements, concerns, etc., and asking for their input. Their awareness is invaluable.

- Spending time in schools and in classrooms; having lunch with staff members on their turf. Classroom teachers, librarians, activity directors, maintainance and operations staff members, office employees all continue to put this activity at the top of their lists of how administrators can become better communicators.
- Inviting district office staff members to the school site at least once a year. It helps their feelings about their jobs when they realize that what they do is very important to what happens with students in classrooms. And, when what you do is more than just a job, it shows.
- Having the school board reaffirm policies and procedures on discipline or student behavior at least every other year and then sharing that information with everyone in the community.
- Having staff recognition activities for years of service, perfect attendance, civic involvement, professional development, etc. Some districts make this a part of a board meeting three or four times a year.
- Scheduling monthly "let's talk it over" sessions with PTA leaders and jointly planning the agenda.
- Sharing budget information and monthly financial statements regularly with all staff members and community leaders. Where this is done, there is little criticism that the district has "plenty of money."
- Asking for input and wanting what you get. One district sent each staff member a small brown bag tied with a piece of yarn. Inside was a penny and a note that said, "A penny for your thoughts on how we can revitalize confidence in our schools."
- Setting up a welcome wagon for your school. Recruit retired teachers or active parents or students as your ambassadors, and have a package of information they can use as they call on new residents.
- Conducting "mini-tours" and special visits for all kinds of groups. Keep them simple and brief.
- Holding "here's what's new" mini-courses for parents about the school curriculum.
- Publishing a curriculum calendar in your local newspaper to advertise what students are learning.
- Using phone calls to invite parents to back-to-school nights and open houses.
- Surveying attendees at parent-teacher conferences to find out what parents would like to know about the school or the district.
- Publishing an information publication about the schools for realtors to use. Most times they'll pay for the printing.
- Trying a workshop for realtors—"To sell the house, sell the schools."
- Encouraging student involvement in the community. For example, the home economics classes in one district took over "meals on wheels" for a week or two. Community response and media coverage were terrific.

- Holding news conferences for student reporters and editors.
- Planning a districtwide course of study on public education—for a day or a week.
- Using other newsletters and newspapers—those put out by churches, service clubs, house organs for local businesses, chambers of commerce, etc. Several schools have even put together packages of "fillers" about their programs for other newsletters to use.
- Spotlighting your good people and good programs.
- Sending lots of notes—after you visit a classroom, when a staff member or student goes that extra mile, for special achievement, etc. Do it by hand on a page from your notepad and give it a really personal touch.
- Sending birthday cards and such. Don't leave it all up to the hospitality committee. A school administrator who cares is very special.
- Getting PTA members and community people to make use of "Letters to the Editor" columns. Those "third-party" testimonials are a definite plus.
- Encouraging teachers to call the homes of students who are absent.
- Being certain "who does what" and "who's responsible for what" is known to all staff members.
- Being visible to your staff members—at least once a day.
- Trying a recorded message line—for staff members or for parents. You can get a lot of important information out in a three-minute message.
- Teaching a class occasionally—or regularly.
- Having an active communications advisory committee. Identify all your publics and do at least one special thing for each at least once a year.
- Creating the kind of environment where staff members are comfortable with you and with each other. First names aren't just the privilege of the top administrator.
- Taking a look at your offices. Do they reflect the positive spirit of public education? Business and personnel staff members like student art displays in their offices, too.

6. Speaking Up for Education

SOMETIMES IT'S EASY to see the need for building confidence in the local school. After all, the more supportive the community, the more likely there will be ample volunteers, enough on-the-job training opportunities and scholarships for students, and a better chance for passage of the next tax bill. It is obvious that positive public relations for the local school is crucial to a successful learning environment for students.

But there is another aspect of the school public relations responsibility: *building confidence in education in general*—or Big Education.

We frequently hear complaints about Big Education: Test scores are down; discipline is bad; kids are not achieving.

All of us share responsibility for building confidence in Big Education. This is an awesome task, but it is also achievable. We may not be able to employ such ad agency strategies as multi-colored printed reports, full-page ads in metropolitan newspapers, or frequent television commercials. But we have a resource that is not available to many institutions hoping to develop public support. That resource is people—teachers, students, parents, graduates, everyone who has some connection with schools.

Recognizing the need to improve Big Education's image and the value of using people to do that, in 1981 NASSP passed this resolution:

> WHEREAS building public confidence in and support for schools is one of education's greatest needs, and
> WHEREAS there are numerous people at each school, including staff, parents and volunteers, that can be formed into a team which speaks on behalf of education, and
> WHEREAS creating such a team is an inexpensive and efficient way to build support for schools, therefore be it
> RESOLVED that NASSP encourage principals and assistant principals to explore ways to inform citizens of education's value and achievements, and be it further
> RESOLVED that secondary school administrators be active in "speaking up" for education at every opportunity.

Who is the individual best able to turn this great resource into an effective confidence-builder? It's the secondary school principal or assistant principal.

Think for a moment of all the people connected with education in your middle level or high school. There are students, administrators, parents, teachers, professional support personnel, district office staff, governing board members, band booster club members, advisory committee representatives, PTA or home-school club members, the football boosters club, community members who regularly attend your athletic events or musicals, volunteers .... The list goes on and on. One researcher indicated that when graduates are added to this list, a high school with an enrollment of 2,000 students has a potential "family" of 38,000 people.

These are all individuals who have some close connection with your school—people who have a reason to support education. They comprise your school's "Education Team." Think of the impact if each of these individuals were to become a spokesperson for your school!

Certainly it's important that newsletters that discuss school programs are sent home, and that presentations are made on school activities, but don't overlook the importance of your Education Team as part of your school's public relations program. Team members go to the grocery store, cocktail parties, the beauty parlor, and church meetings; they belong to a bridge club or tennis club. At any of these places a member of your Education Team could be asked a question about your school or Big Education. That's an opportunity to speak up for education—to build public confidence.

We can start building an Education Team without spending a great deal of money or time. And it can have a great impact. Principals and assistant principals have contact with many members of the Education Team, and can encourage these people to speak up for education.

Unfortunately, we have not done a good job in the past of telling the people closest to the profession about its values and achievements. One school public relations person tells the story of keynoting a back-to-school staff orientation with a 20-minute presentation titled, "What's Right with Education." Afterward, a teacher who had been in education for about five years came up and said, "No one has ever told me before that it's important to work in education; that education is important to our society."

Principals can have a positive impact on assuring that teachers, professional support staff members, and volunteers are positive spokespersons whenever they are asked about schools. Principals and assistant principals must see that those individuals feel committed to speaking up and that they have the information to do so.

Schools and students will receive a side benefit from this: If we help people understand that they are involved in a profession that truly is crucial to our democratic way of life, they will have more *pride in their performance.*

How do principals tackle the task of building a team to speak up for Big Education? Here are some suggestions. (NASSP has provided some in its publications and will continue to do so.)

You can find much to be proud of right in your school. Devote a portion of a staff meeting to brainstorming the successes of your school in recent years. Look at student awards, staff achievements, and contributions that students have made to your community. Has one of your young people won a state speaking contest? How many of your students have earned scholarships? Has one of your teachers or professional support people been recognized for outstanding effort by a local club or professional group? Have your students worked at a convalescent home, cleaned up a dry creek bed, or performed some other community service? All of these are accomplishments of which your school can be proud.

Don't stop there! Put those successes in writing. One school district collects all its positive newspaper clippings during the year and reproduces them in a packet for distribution to staff members in September. It's a great way to refresh everyone's memory about the accomplishments of the previous school year.

It might be valuable to send a list of successes to your local legislators. Those individuals make important decisions about our profession, and we should make certain they understand what we are doing well. Everyone on the Education Team would benefit be receiving a list of your local successes.

Once you have developed that information, look for ways to share it. Here are just a few suggestions:

- *Coffee Klatches*. There's nothing new about coffee klatches, but they are an effective way to deliver your message to those who no longer have young people in school. Adults without school-age children today number slightly more than 75 percent of our adult population. Even though they no longer have children in school, they pay taxes, vote, and deserve to know what is happening in schools.

- *Placemats*. Every community has civic groups that hold breakfast or luncheon meetings. Some educational groups print placemats with local accomplishments listed under the heading "What's Right with Our Schools." Those placemats are offered to organizations holding breakfast, luncheon, or dinner meetings.

- *Lunch Menus*. One of the best-read publications in many homes is the school lunch menu, especially if parents hang it on their kitchen bulletin board. Squeeze in some information about your successes. Do the same with other publications that are well read.

- *School Vehicles*. Have you ever noticed that commercial buses carry placards advertising a product? Why can't school vehicles do the same? As mentioned previously, the Topeka, Kans. school district's fleet of 60 trucks—which carry school lunches, mail, and maintenance crews—also carry posters proclaiming the successes of the schools.

- *Announcement Boards*. Many high schools that have announcement boards use them only to indicate dates of the upcoming football game or open house. Burbank (Calif.) High School uses its board to communicate accomplishments to the public. One sign read "Burbank High Students Had Record High Basic Skills Scores." It also reported the number of scholarship winners.

- *Public Speaking.* Look for opportunities to tell people about your accomplishments. Ann Barkelew, public information officer for the Los Angeles County Schools, carries with her a prepared speech on the achievements of schools in her county. We all occasionally go to meetings that feature breakfast or luncheon speakers, who sometimes are delayed or can't attend. No one would rather hear a 20-minute presentation on what schools are doing well than a program chairperson who has just learned the scheduled speaker is lost. In a one-year period, Ann gave her presentation five or six times in just such situations.

There are many opportunities to communicate the value of education, and principals are the key to developing the education team that will speak up for education.

7. The Name of the Game Is Common Sense

PERHAPS THE MOST important part of school public relations is using common sense. People are going to form an image of your school based on their experiences with you, your staff, and your students. Every time you answer a telephone, chat with a parent, or meet with anyone, you have the opportunity to build support for your school and for education—if you use common sense. If you don't, you may create a negative image.

Ask yourself how you would feel if you were the recipient of messages you have been delivering recently. Put yourself in the place of parents, students, or staff members.

An example of a lack of common sense involved Mr. and Mrs. Jones, parents of fifth and third grade students, who moved into a new school district. Initially, the Joneses were very impressed with the school's communications—primarily the principal's newsletter, which arrived home every Friday afternoon with much useful information. One Friday in April the principal wrote that the school was about to make student-teacher assignments for the following year, and that parents would have the opportunity to request a specific teacher for their child. To do so, the newsletter read, parents should fill out a request form that would be available at the parent-teacher conferences the following week.

The Joneses attended the conference, and the first thing they asked for was a teacher request form. The teacher responded, "What's that?" After the conference, they went to the school office and asked the secretary for a teacher request form. A similar response was given before a volunteer in the office indicated that they were in the file cabinet in the corner.

A week later, armed with the form, the Joneses phoned the principal and asked who would be teaching sixth and fourth grades the following year so they could fill out their forms. The principal indicated that grade assignments were not yet determined. The Joneses thought it was odd that this "opportunity" to request a teacher was advertised, yet grade assignments hadn't been made yet. They thanked the principal for the opportunity and promised to call back.

A second phone call followed in May, when again the parents were told the decision hadn't yet been made. When the parents called once again, during the first week of June, the principal indicated that the student-teacher assignments for the following year had been made the previous afternoon.

37

That principal could send out a slick, multi-colored newsletter every other day from that point on, but the communications that Mr. and Mrs. Jones are most likely to remember is their experience with the teacher request form. That's how opinions are formed. That's PR without common sense.

There are many opportunities to use common sense. One of the most frequent opportunities is when answering the telephone. The only exposure many people have with the school is via the telephone, and how phone calls are handled will determine whether those people have a good or a negative impression.

Whenever someone phones one high school in Tennessee, the caller is greeted by, "Thank you for calling the best high school in Tennessee." That certainly sets a tone for the conversation and is far better than the "Yes?" that is heard at other schools.

Using students on the school switchboard is another creative approach that also can be a good experience for them. But it's critical that students be trained before taking on this task—trained in using common sense.

Just as important as answering the telephone is greeting visitors when they arrive on the school campus. What's the first thing that visitors see at the entrance to many schools throughout the country? It's a welcome sign that reads: "All visitors must register at the office. Violators will be prosecuted." That approach hardly makes one feel at home. And often visitors are not even directed to the office.

One high school used common sense in greeting visitors. The school's woodworking and art classes combined to create a sign that reads, "Welcome to Noname High School. Please register at the office." A map is posted below the sign.

If your school is fortunate enough to have a sign that actually helps people find the office, how they are met and what they see in that office will also build an opinion. Upon entering one intermediate school office, I was immediately told by the school secretary that gum chewing was not allowed on campus. As soon as I opened the door at another school, a secretary left her desk, came to me, and asked how she could help. Those two experiences led to two totally different opinions about the schools.

Another blunder is the so-called "humorous" sign that hangs from walls or sits on desks. One secretary displayed a sign on her desk that asked, "How can you soar like an eagle when you are surrounded by turkeys?" That may bring a chuckle, but it can communicate a negative message in the minds of some people. We don't need to send messages like that.

Common sense techniques are perhaps the easiest part of a school public relations program to implement. They include caring about people and thinking about their feelings. They mean saying "thank you" for a job well done. They mean learning the names of students and chatting with them in the halls. They mean remembering that people are

38

constantly receiving messages from your school and trying to make those messages positive ones.

Principals and assistant principals are responsible for working with staff members to assure that *everyone* knows the importance of using common sense.

8. Can a Reporter Be Your Friend?

DO ALL NEWSPAPER and television reporters have one gigantic eye in the middle of their forehead? Do they always growl when they speak? Are they always out to get you?

Many educators believe that the press always reports bad news about education. Sometimes that is the case when problems occur; but positive news can also be—and is—reported.

The press *can* report the positive news. Sometimes that doesn't happen because no one informs the press about the good news. If there is a riot on your school campus, it's likely that reporters will find out about it. If an outstanding classroom activity is taking place, you will probably have to take the initiative to let them know.

If you wish to develop a positive media relations program for your school, you must first find out whether your district has a public relations or public information professional on staff. If so, get to know that person and find out how you can work with him or her to gain coverage for your school. Let that person know you are willing to work with the media and that you have some activities that might interest the press. Make certain you understand the program your public information professional has developed so you are not working at cross purposes.

School public relations people have the skills to write news releases that the press will use, and they should also have a relationship with the local reporters that will bring attention to the material they submit. But they, too, will probably need your ideas about activities that are potential positive stories, since they cannot be aware of every school activity in the district.

If your school system does not have a public information person, you can still work with the media if you follow a few simple guidelines.

A good first step is simply to pick up the telephone and set up a meeting with the editor or reporter who covers your school. Don't wait until a riot or other negative incident to meet the reporter. Let that first meeting be on a positive note. You may want to discuss the goals of your school, your philosophy of education, or even some successful programs. Ask the reporter how you might be helpful. Find out if the reporter would like you to provide some story ideas, and what type of stories he or she would like.

Also let the reporter know that you are willing to serve as a resource—when the reporter has a question about education, you would be willing to answer it. Educators sometimes complain that newspapers print inaccurate information about schools, but education is a fairly complicated business. A reporter who is just starting on the education beat has a lot to learn, and we can help.

Here are some more tips for working with reporters.

- Always be honest. Sometimes it's easy to respond to a question with a half-truth, but that could kill your credibility for years to come. In the long run, you will get more positive coverage if you build a relationship of honesty with reporters—even if that means a negative story now and then.
- Prepare a list of story ideas from your school. Reporters generally have too much territory to cover to know the latest developments everywhere in their assignment area. A good focus is instructional activities. Do you have a project that is new, that uses unusual equipment, that involves the community, that adopts a new approach to teaching a traditional subject? All are story possibilities. You might brainstorm some story ideas with your staff and then suggest them to your reporters.
- Don't be disappointed if not all your ideas are used. Remember, you are competing with many other institutions and individuals. Keep trying.
- Keep your head about errors. If there is a mistake in a story, don't phone the reporter's boss and make a federal case out of it. The error may not even have negated the thrust of the story. A calm, low-key phone call to the reporter, to ensure that the mistake won't happen again, is appropriate.
- Don't be afraid to be interviewed. A professional reporter will not knowingly misquote anyone. Education, however, can be complicated to people not involved in it every day. So take the necessary time to explain the situation. If you are not willing to talk with reporters your story probably will not be told.
- Respect the reporter's needs. Deadlines are inflexible for the media. You don't need to drop everything for the press, but perhaps you can spare a few minutes or have someone else respond.
- Use the resources you have. If you have a journalism program, perhaps some of the advanced students could prepare releases on student awards, music and drama programs, open houses, or other events at school. They could even do occasional "personality features" on students or staff members. Such activity gets the news releases written and gives your journalism students experience working with the professional media.
- Don't forget the radio station news broadcasts. Radio can be an important media for communicating the school's story. A phone call to the news director of your local radio station could result in a big payoff. Ask if he or she is interested in news from your

42

school. Provide some story ideas. If a station is interested, interviews can be conducted right over the telephone.

- It's important that you treat all media representatives equally. Don't give an exclusive story to one reporter. Don't give a story earlier to one reporter than to the others. That will make enemies very quickly. If a reporter calls you and initiates a story, don't call all the others with that "scoop." Generally, a "scoop" remains just that until you have received four inquiries about it. At that point you can assume it's general knowledge, and distribute your own news release on the topic.

This chapter concludes with three articles that will help you build a positive program with the press. The first, "The World's Shortest Course in Educational Journalism," deals with writing a news release. If your district has a public relations professional, check with that person. If not, this short course will help.

Letters to the editor are an important way to communicate. The article written by Samuel L. Zimmerman, a former vice president of the National School Public Relations Association, deals with responding to negative letters. The third article, reprinted from NASSP's *Building Public Confidence,* focuses on letters to the editor that communicate the positive news of education.

The World's Shortest Course in Educational Journalism

Developed by Gayle Wayne

1. Type your story on one side of the paper only, using 8½ × 11″ paper.
2. Double space.
3. Leave the top third of the first page blank, except for source information.
4. Source information should be placed in the top left corner of the first page and should include:
   - The full name and address of your organization (school)
   - The writer's name
   - A telephone number (night and day if necessary) where the writer can be reached.
5. End each page with a complete paragraph.
6. Make it short. If a second page is necessary, always indicate "MORE" at the bottom of the first page.
7. Use any of the following marks to indicate the end of the story: ###   -30-   XXX   ***
8. Leave generous margins all around.
9. Consider the deadlines of the local press when planning and writing your story. Get the story in as far in advance as possible.
10. Send the news to your local reporter, by name.
11. Always use first and last names, and identify every person mentioned.
12. Go easy on the adjectives.
13. Use short words, short sentences, short paragraphs.
14. If you don't see your story in print when you expect it, ONE follow-up call to the reporter is acceptable. Find out why it didn't run. You may learn something that will help you next time.

When editors cut a story because of space limits, they begin at the bottom of your story. The following is an example of the order your story should follow:

44

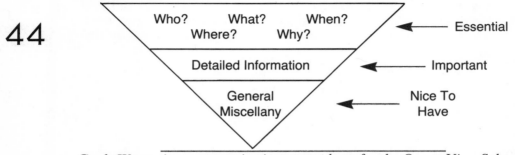

Gayle Wayne is a communications consultant for the Ocean View School District in Huntington Beach, Calif.

Dealing with "Ugly" Letters to the Editor

By Samuel L. Zimmerman

One of the most difficult areas of media relations for educators is dealing with so-called "ugly" (or negative) letters to the editor, written by irate and often ill-informed citizens. Such letters can address a variety of topics ranging from lack of discipline or busing for racial balance to demands for a return to prayer in the schools. Denunciations of bond levies are another common topic for letter writers.

When I discussed the ugly letter problem with school public relations people from across the country, I found a single theme in their advice. Their common reaction was "do not create a major continuing news story from what began as a letter read by only a limited audience."

Overreaction can, and all too often does, blow such letters into full-scale newspaper articles, prominently displayed and read by an audience many times larger than the audience that read the original letter.

Here are some do's and don'ts to keep in mind when you are faced by an editorial page containing an ugly letter about your school district.

Don'ts

- Don't forget to use restraint. Colleagues can sometimes push you into a situation in which your staff members become unwilling newsmakers because of an ugly letter.
- Don't try to do battle with extremist groups. There is little hope of changing their attitudes. Peer pressure from proschool leaders is the best way to deal with such groups. Use interpersonal relations, not written replies to the newspapers.
- Don't refrain from calling on someone outside the school family if you feel a reply must be made. Ghostwrite the letter if necessary, but have someone from the community who agrees with the approach and content of the letter sign it.
- Don't try to deal with complex issues in a single letter; you'll only lose credibility.
- Don't run the risk of generating public sympathy for the underdog by attacking the letter writer.
- Don't expect editors to automatically take your side. Be prepared with ample information refuting any charges contained in the letter.

45

Do's

- Develop an information story or news release about the "ugly" letter, but do not repeat any of the charges.

Samuel L. Zimmerman is school-community relations director for the Greenville (S.C.) County School District.

- Provide the facts regarding any charges or claims presented in ugly letters to key internal and external communicators.
- Make a factual response only as a final resort, and back your response with explicit figures. Have the president of the board of education or the superintendent sign the response. Stick to the facts—don't get into a philosophical or defensive posture.
- Visit with the publisher/editor and attempt to get an editorial response added at the bottom of a rebuttal letter. Provide factual information to make the response.

Share Your Thoughts—Write Letters-to-Editors

Principals can have a positive impact on the coverage of education in newspapers. All papers include letters to the editor. Some people only pen such letters when they are irritated, but letters can also be a way to share positive thoughts about schools.

Consider suggesting to advisory councils, booster clubs, or student councils that they devote the last five minutes of their meetings to having members write letters to the editor.

Letters could reflect the importance of education to our society; what education has meant to an adult now content with his or her lifestyle; what the local school has contributed to its community; reflections on the school's learning program; contributions school staff members have made; or the need for a community to pull together in support of its schools.

Reflections on the annual Gallup Poll would be an appropriate topic for a letter. Do members of the council believe that education is crucial to a person's success in life? How do they feel about the performance of education compared to other institutions?

Here are some tips on writing letters to the editor:
- Don't make letters too long. One to one-and-a-half, double-spaced, typewritten pages is fine. Deal with one or two main points.
- Newspapers generally will accept hand-written letters, but they must be done very neatly. Printing is better than writing. Typewritten letters are best.
- Don't be disappointed if your first letter isn't used. Keep trying. Newspapers receive many, many letters and can't use them all.
- It's fine to send the same letter to more than one newspaper. But if you do that, don't send an original to one paper and a carbon copy to another. Or don't send your letter to one paper on Monday and to the other the following Friday. Treat all newspapers equally, and they are much more likely to treat you well.
- Understand deadlines. They are inflexible. Individual papers have different deadlines, but if the paper is published on Thursday, don't turn in a letter on Wednesday and expect to see it in the Thursday edition. Call the newspaper office to determine the deadlines.
- Don't complain if your letter isn't used right away, or if it is altered slightly. Editors are paid to edit, and most of them will help you communicate the message.

47

Reprinted from the October 1980 issue of "Building Public Confidence," supplement to the NASSP Newsletter.

9. What Do I Do on Monday, And Where Do I Get Help?

THE PREVIOUS PAGES have dealt with the importance of positive school public relations, and with a number of practical ways to achieve that goal.

Now comes a caution: School public relations is a long-term proposition. No matter how hard a person tries, or how talented he or she may be, images cannot be turned around overnight, in a few days, or in a few weeks. So take pride in the small successes you may have initially in building public confidence.

It is far better to select a few proven school public relations ideas and gradually implement them in your schools than to try to do everything mentioned in this monograph next week. Evaluate your local information needs, your community, your financial resources, and the talents of your staff along with the suggestions in this book. You are the best judge of what your community needs and what will work best for your community.

Use the following checklist to help in reviewing the most important aspects of a school public. The more items you are able to check off, the more skilled a communicator you will have become. And you should see more support building for your school and a greater feeling of pride among students and staff.

Have you:

☐ Read a publication explaining school public relations.
☐ Explained the importance of school public relations to your staff.
☐ Identified the internal and external publics with which you deal.
☐ Identified the people who communicate for you.
☐ Evaluated how effective your school's morning announcements are and improved them if necessary.
☐ Established a student communications council, if appropriate.
☐ Developed a staff bulletin.
☐ Scheduled regular staff meetings to which all staff members are invited.
☐ Established ways to inform volunteers.
☐ Developed procedures to thank volunteers.
☐ Conducted a search to determine the information needs of your various publics.

49

- ☐ Developed a school newsletter that is mailed home on a regular basis.
- ☐ Communicated to your staff that the best way to build a positive image is by doing a good job.
- ☐ Identified the perceptions people hold about your school.
- ☐ Developed a communications plan.
- ☐ Met your district public relations professional, if there is one.
- ☐ Identified possible news stories at your school.
- ☐ Determined what would be appropriate public service announcements for your school and asked local radio and television people for help in producing them.
- ☐ Introduced yourself to the news director at community radio stations and inquired about possible news coverage.
- ☐ Determined if you are sending your staff bulletin to everyone who could benefit from reading it.
- ☐ Set up a network of key communicators.
- ☐ Established a systematic program of sending students into the community to perform.
- ☐ Developed a Golden Age Card program, or something similar, for senior citizens.
- ☐ Considered building a volunteer program as part of your school public relations efforts.
- ☐ Encouraged student reporters to develop material about your school for the professional press.
- ☐ Established programs in which your students provide tutoring assistance to elementary youngsters.
- ☐ Prepared a speech you can use with civic groups and sought the chance to present it.
- ☐ Established a way for people to have their questions about your school answered.
- ☐ Used your marquee or other such boards to communicate your important messages.
- ☐ Assured that telephones are answered and visitors greeted in a pleasant manner.
- ☐ Developed a theme for your school.
- ☐ Established ways for positive telephone calls to be made to parents.
- ☐ Brainstormed with your staff accomplishments of the school and put those on paper.
- ☐ Printed and distributed placemats featuring the value and accomplishments of schools.
- ☐ Evaluated the common sense you use in communicating with people.
- ☐ Developed a "welcome sign" that delivers a positive greeting.
- ☐ Met the newspaper reporter or editor who covers your area.
- ☐ Set up ways to have letters-to-the-editor written.
- ☐ Evaluated your public relations efforts at the end of the year.

These tasks may seem monumental, but help can be had. The following school public relations materials are available through NASSP.

NASSP Materials for Communicating Education's Successes

"What's Right with Secondary Schools!" This resource card listing education's successes can be given to teachers, professional support staff, parents, club members, and others. Serves as a quick reference.

Inservice Materials (Tapes of presentations made at the 1981 NASSP Convention.)

"School Public Relations—It's Everyone's Job" by Ann Barkelew, public information officer, Los Angeles County Superintendent of Schools Office. Focuses on ways to build community support for schools. Available as video or audiotape.

"Public Relations Principles for Prnicipals of Larger Schools" by Ann Barkelew. Looks at specific ways principals can communicate their school's message. Audiotape.

"The Principal: Key To Building Public Confidence in Schools" by Lew Armistead, public information officer, National Association of Secondary School Principals. Reviews how principals can build a team of people who will speak up for education. Audiotape.

"Public Relations Ideas That Work in Schools" by John Kicklighter, principal, Lakeside High School, Atlanta, Ga. Suggests specific practical public relations ideas for schools. Audiotape.

"Change and Community Support" by Burma Lockridge, principal; Linda Hopping and Becky Vaughn, Title IV-C, coordinators, Sandy Springs Middle School, Atlanta, Ga. Focuses on maintaining community support during times of change. Audiotape.

"What's Right About American Education" by William Georgiades, dean, School of Education, University of Houston. Discusses the successes of schools in America. Audiotape.

Other Resources

NASSP Bulletin, January 1979. Twelve articles on various aspects of building-level public relations.

More Help

Another outstanding source of information and materials on school public relations is the National School Public Relations Association (NSPRA), the only such organization specializing in school communications. NSPRA is located at 1801 North Moore St., Arlington, Va. 22209, (703) 528-5840. NSPRA also has state chapters that can provide speakers and consultant help. A list of state chapter presidents is available through the NSPRA national office, along with a complete listing of its services.

A Final Word

School public relations is a new activity for many educators. But we do it all the time whether we know it or not. With a little planning and some occasional help, you can develop a positive school public relations program. You can build a positive image for your school and education in general.

NASSP is anxious to provide the help. Good luck!

52

ABOUT THE AUTHOR: Lew Armistead is NASSP's director of public information.